Burmese Proverbs and Sayings

AUTHOR : Timeless Edition

Introduction

Proverbs are often figurative formulas, expressing a truth of experience or advice of practical wisdom.

With this book, you will discover these truths and advice of Burmese wisdom which will undoubtedly allow you to discover a glimpse of Burmese culture.

The official language of Myanmar is **Burmese** (also known as **Myanmar**). It is used in government, education, and media, and serves as the lingua franca of the country. Burmese is spoken by the majority of the population, though there are also many ethnic groups with their own languages.

Discover also our full proverbs collection books on our Amazon author section.

We will now let you read this exceptional and unique book.

Enjoy

Burmese Proverbs with *Original Text*, *Translation* and their *Meaning* .

1. **Original Text:**
   "မိုးရွာပြီးနောက်တပျိုးနင်းခြင်း"

   - *Translation*: "After the rain, plow the field."

   - *Meaning* : This proverb emphasizes the importance of taking action at the right time. After a period of difficulty (rain), one should take advantage of the good times (plowing the field) to make progress.

2. **Original Text:**
   "သီးပွင့်အောင်လှုပ်ရှားပါစေ"

   - *Translation*: "Let the fruit bloom with effort."

   - *Meaning* : Success comes with hard work and effort. Just as a fruit tree requires care to bear fruit, a person must put in effort to succeed.

3. Original Text:

"ခါးလျှောက်ခွင်းမက်တိုင်"

- ○ **_Translation_**: "The snake does not make a noise unless it strikes."

- ○ **_Meaning_** : This suggests that people who are quiet or reserved are often not to be underestimated; their silence can be a sign of strength or careful planning.

4. Original Text:

"စိတ်ရောဂါရှိသော်လည်းကျန်းမာတယ်"

- ○ **_Translation_**: "Though you have a mental illness, your body remains healthy."

- ○ **_Meaning_** : This proverb means that sometimes

external appearances may be fine, but internal struggles or challenges might exist that are hidden from the outside world.

5. **Original Text:**

"ဝေဖန်မှုတွေ့လျှင်ရှုမကြည့်ပါ"

- *Translation*: "When criticized, do not look at it directly."

- *Meaning* : This suggests that people should not dwell on criticism but rather move forward without focusing too much on negative comments.

6. **Original Text:**

"ထီးမြှင့်တယ်ဆိုရင်ကျောင်းအပေါ်မလှမ်းပါ"

- *Translation*: "If the umbrella is raised, don't reach for the temple."

- *Meaning* : This proverb encourages people to focus

on one goal at a time and avoid distractions. If you're already prepared (with an umbrella), don't go after things that aren't relevant at the moment.

7. **Original Text:**

"ကြောင်အိပ်နေချိန်မှာငါးမုန်တိုင်းထွက်မလာ"

- ○ **_Translation_**: "The cat doesn't catch fish while it's sleeping."

- ○ **_Meaning_** : You can't achieve your goals if you're not actively working toward them. Success requires effort and action.

8. **Original Text:**

"နာလန်တမင်းရဲ့လက်ဖက်သီးဟာမျက်နှာကြီး"

- ○ **_Translation_**: "The bitter gourd of the great king is still bitter."

- ○ **_Meaning_** : This suggests that no matter how

powerful or important someone is, they cannot change certain truths or inherent qualities, just as the bitter gourd remains bitter despite any external influence.

9. **Original Text:**
"ကျွဲစွတ်သီးရသောအခါမှာငါးလိုပါ"

   - ***Translation***: "When the cow is fed, the fish are caught."

   - ***Meaning*** : This highlights the importance of resources and the need to invest in the right things to see progress in other areas.

10. **Original Text:**
"ထီးမကြီးရင်လောင်ဖို့လဲမရှိ"

- ***Translation***: "If the umbrella isn't big enough, it won't cover you from the rain."

- **_Meaning_ :** This implies that you can't expect to be shielded from something if you don't have the right resources or preparation.

11. Original Text:

"အိုးတစ်လုံးကိုအေးကာမပြန်တက်"

- **_Translation_:** "A pot that's not yet boiled won't rise again."

- **_Meaning_ :** When something isn't ready, it can't succeed. Preparation is key before attempting something.

12. Original Text:

"အိပ်ခန်းရဲ့ပန်းခွက်ကိုနင်ရင်း"

- **_Translation_:** "When the flower pot is carried, the flower gets crushed."

- **_Meaning_ :** This suggests that when things are handled carelessly, even the best outcomes can be ruined by improper handling.

13. Original Text:

"တစ်ချိန်တည်းမှာမြေပေါ်လှည့်မပြေး"

- *Translation*: "One cannot run around the ground at the same time."

- *Meaning* : It advises that one must focus on one task or goal at a time for effective results.

14. Original Text:

"အမီးအိမ်တော်မှာရေခဲတွေနံမကိုင်ပါ"

- *Translation*: "Don't hold ice water inside a house of flames."

- *Meaning* : This means that trying to apply something in the wrong place or context will lead to failure.

15. Original Text: "အလှူချင်းကမလား"

- *Translation*: "The person who offers the charity may not expect the blessing."

- ***Meaning*** : When you give, don't always expect something in return. True generosity is selfless.

16. Original Text:

"သူရောတိုင်ကိုကိုးအောင်သင့်ကိုမရ"

- ***Translation***: "He who supports the bridge cannot cross it."

- ***Meaning*** : Sometimes, the person who helps or supports others does not benefit from the same actions themselves.

17. Original Text:

"သီလလဲမပြည့်တော့လမ်းပြန်ချင်လွန်း"

- ***Translation***: "Though the moon is full, it wants to grow again."

- ***Meaning*** : Even when people achieve something, they still long for more. It highlights human nature to always seek improvement.

18. Original Text:

"အပူလှိုင်းမှာခါးဖို့ဖြစ်"

- *Translation*: "One must endure the heat to extract the gold."

- *Meaning* : Success requires effort and sacrifice; only through enduring difficulties can one achieve something valuable.

19. Original Text:

"ငါးငါးရေထဲတက်သွားတယ်"

- *Translation*: "The fish went up to the sky."

- *Meaning* : A rare or impossible event, representing something unlikely to happen.

20. Original Text:

"တံတားနဲ့ထူသောပစ္စည်းတွေအဆင့်"

- *Translation*: "The materials used in building the bridge will last long."

- **_Meaning_ :** When a foundation is strong and well-prepared, the results will endure over time.

21. **Original Text:**

"လှည့်စားနေချိန်မှာလမ်းမကြီး"

- **_Translation_:** "While spinning, the road turns wide."

- **_Meaning_ :** A challenge can seem bigger than it is when you are stuck in a difficult moment, but it often becomes easier as time passes.

22. **Original Text:**

"မျက်နှာတစ်လုံးမှာမီးမောင်"

- **_Translation_:** "A flame on a single face."

- **_Meaning_ :** Refers to a person who is full of energy or passion but might not be able to focus this energy constructively.

23. Original Text:
"ဆယ်ကျော်သတ်ကလှမ်းအလို"

- *Translation*: "The ten-year-old will look up for guidance."

- *Meaning* : A younger person or someone inexperienced will naturally seek the wisdom of the elders or more experienced individuals.

24. Original Text:
"ရေကူးရက်အပေါ်ပြောင်းနေတယ်"

- *Translation*: "The current flows, but it always changes."

- *Meaning* : Change is inevitable, and it teaches that you need to adapt to the changing circumstances of life.

25. Original Text:
"အတွင်းမီးတိုကိုရှာဖွေ"

- *Translation*: "Seek the internal flame."

- **_Meaning_ :** The answer lies within yourself. It suggests self-reliance and introspection.

26. Original Text:
"လယ်ယာအမျိုးသမီးထမင်းရောက်မှာ"

- **_Translation_:** "A farmer's wife can only dream of rice."

- **_Meaning_ :** This suggests that people from humble backgrounds often have to work harder to achieve things others take for granted.

27. Original Text:
"တိုင်ပတ်စရာတံခါးတင်နား"

- **_Translation_:** "The gate closes when it has a post."

- **_Meaning_ :** Sometimes, the opportunities are not available until the conditions are met. Everything has its timing.

28. Original Text:
"ပြည်သူမရှုးရင်မေတ္တာကရှုး"

- *Translation*: "The full moon may shine even brighter."

- *Meaning* : This proverb speaks about growth and improvement: even when you're at your best, there's still room to shine brighter.

29. Original Text:
"သင်္ကြန်ကိုင်တော်ပုံကြို"

- *Translation*: "The lion takes its final stand on the peak."

- *Meaning* : This represents the idea that a true leader or person of power shows their greatness at the moment of final challenge.

30. Original Text:
"ချိုးကလေးအလိုအကြား"

- *Translation*: "The young child's hands grasp."

- ***Meaning*** : This implies that children or inexperienced individuals often try to hold on to everything, often not understanding the weight or importance of their actions.

31. **Original Text:** "အမဲသွားမလိုလားရ"

- ***Translation***: "The cow does not long for the wheat."

- ***Meaning*** : This means that different people have different desires and needs. What works for one may not be the same for another.

32. **Original Text:**
"ငှက်တောင်နေသော်လည်းသံတွေအတွင်း"

- ***Translation***: "Even the bird is trapped within its own cage."

- ***Meaning*** : This suggests that sometimes, even those who seem free or powerful can be trapped by their own circumstances or choices.

33. Original Text: "အချိန်မီနားမလည်"

- *Translation*: "The bell rings, but no one listens."

- *Meaning* : A missed opportunity, suggesting that even when opportunities arise, people may not be aware or prepared for them.

34. Original Text: "ရွှေတံဆိပ်မထွက်မှုသွား"

- *Translation*: "The gold spoon doesn't leave the bowl."

- *Meaning* : This speaks to those who are born with privilege or success, emphasizing that some things are always with you due to circumstances.

35. Original Text: "ကြီးထွားမှုကိုဖောက်ထွင်းပါ"

- *Translation*: "Break through to growth."

- _**Meaning**_ : This proverb suggests that true growth comes from overcoming challenges and barriers, and personal development comes with effort.

36. Original Text:
"စပျစ်ပင်ဖုံးကြီးတော်"

- _**Translation**_: "The vine climbs high."

- _**Meaning**_ : It signifies the idea of achieving great heights, often implying that even modest beginnings can lead to significant achievements.

37. Original Text:
"အရွယ်ထူပြီးတဲ့အခါ"

- _**Translation**_: "When the age is fixed, it doesn't change."

- _**Meaning**_ : Time and aging are inevitable, and there are things beyond one's control that can't be reversed.

38. Original Text:
"မြေလှမ်းထွက်ပေါက်ငွေ"

- *Translation*: "The road opens, and the money follows."

- *Meaning* : Good efforts or decisions lead to prosperity or rewards, suggesting that when opportunities arise, wealth or success will follow.

39. Original Text: "ငါးပိတစ်ခုလုံး"

- *Translation*: "A whole fish at once."

- *Meaning* : This speaks about handling large challenges all at once. Sometimes, it's better to break tasks into smaller pieces instead of taking on too much at once.

40. Original Text:
"လယ်ယာပြားထိုးပြီး"

- *__Translation__*: "The field is plowed before planting."

- *__Meaning__* : Preparation is essential before any task. You must lay the groundwork before beginning a project for it to succeed.

41. Original Text:
"စဉ်းစားမယ်ဆိုရင်ရှုပ်ထွေး"

- *__Translation__*: "When you overthink, it becomes complicated."

- *__Meaning__* : Overthinking or complicating things can hinder progress. It suggests that simplicity and clear thinking are key.

42. Original Text:
"အလင်းရောင်တိုးတက်"

- *__Translation__*: "The light grows brighter."

- *__Meaning__* : Progress and clarity come with time. This implies that as you learn and grow, you become wiser or more enlightened.

43. Original Text:

"ရွှေတုံးရည်နဲ့မမြစ်မချ"

- **_Translation_**: "A gold coin will not melt in water."

- **_Meaning_** : This speaks to the idea of unchangeable qualities. Some things or people cannot be altered by external forces or challenges.

44. Original Text:

"အပြည်ပြည်ဆိုင်ရာထောင်မှန်း"

- **_Translation_**: "From city to city, there is unity."

- **_Meaning_** : This suggests that no matter where you go, unity or commonality can be found among people, culture, or understanding.

45. Original Text: "ပြန်ဆွဲထားခြင်းရသ"

- **_Translation_**: "What is tied must be untied."

- *Meaning* : Everything has its time. Just as knots are tied and untied, challenges are temporary and will eventually be resolved.

46. Original Text:

"မေတ္တာကစားချင်းတော်"

- *Translation*: "Kindness brings out the best."

- *Meaning* : Through acts of kindness, you bring out the goodness in others, highlighting the value of compassion in creating harmony.

47. Original Text:

"ငါးအိုးကိုတင်တန်းစွမ်း"

- *Translation*: "The fish bowl is carefully balanced."

- *Meaning* : Small things can have a great impact, and careful balance is needed to maintain harmony in life or situations.

48. Original Text:

"ဆူးတောက်တောကတုံဆွဲ"

- *Translation*: "The hoe moves the soil."

- *Meaning* : This speaks to how hard work or effort can move obstacles or challenges, representing persistence.

49. Original Text: "လယ်ယာရင်းအချိန်"

- *Translation*: "The time for farming is now."

- *Meaning* : Timing is crucial in life and business. This suggests that you must take action at the right moment to succeed.

50. Original Text:

"အာနိသင်ဖောက်ထွင်း"

- *Translation*: "Unveil the mystery."

- *Meaning* : Encourages seeking the truth or solving complex issues.

Everything has its secrets waiting to be uncovered.

51. Original Text:

"သိုးတစ်ကောင်ကိုတိုးထွက်"

- *Translation*: "The sheep will grow up."

- *Meaning* : It implies that growth happens gradually and that progress is inevitable with time.

52. Original Text:

"လျှပ်စစ်နည်းမပျောက်"

- *Translation*: "The electric current never disappears."

- *Meaning* : This emphasizes that true energy or power is constant and will always find a way to flow or work.

53. Original Text:

"မြစ်ရဲ့အမည်ကိုသိအောင်ပွား"

- *Translation*: "The river's name is known by its course."

- *Meaning* : The true nature of something can be understood by how it behaves or progresses.

54. Original Text: "နတ်မယ်ရယ်မှ အဆောက်အအုံကွဲ"

- *Translation*: "Even the god's house has cracks."

- *Meaning* : No one or nothing is perfect; flaws and imperfections exist everywhere, even in the highest places.

55. Original Text: "လမ်းစစ်မှတ်ရှိသောသူမှတ်"

- *Translation*: "The one who sees the road knows the way."

- *Meaning* : The person who is familiar with the path or journey is the one who can lead others effectively.

56. Original Text: "ရှက်တစ်ခုပြီးတယ်"

- *Translation*: "The leaf has already fallen."

- *Meaning* : It's about accepting things that are beyond your control, particularly when something has already happened and cannot be undone.

57. Original Text: "ဝါယမစ်ဂျုံချို"

- *Translation*: "The owl doesn't fly without purpose."

- *Meaning* : Everything we do has a purpose or reason behind it. There's always intent behind actions.

58. Original Text: "ပန်းနာယပ်ထက်ခြောက်"

- *Translation*: "The flower withers when it's pressed."

- *Meaning* : This refers to how external pressure can diminish potential. It advises to avoid unnecessary pressure.

59. Original Text: "ပြည့်စုံမှသာပြု"

- *Translation*: "Only when full does one act."

- *Meaning* : You cannot act effectively until you're ready. Preparation and completion are required for success.

60. Original Text: "ပေါင်တောင်ရေလို"

- *Translation*: "The river is like the shore."

- *Meaning* : This suggests that all things are interconnected, and where one exists, the other is sure to follow.

61. Original Text: "မှောင်မိုက်သကေ့တသတ်"

- *Translation*: "A dark moon guides the way."

- *Meaning* : Even in difficult times, there's always hope and guidance if one is persistent enough to find it.

62. Original Text:

"အဆက်အရာမှပေးခြင်း"

- *Translation*: "Giving from the heart is a chain."

- *Meaning* : Genuine acts of kindness create a ripple effect. When one person gives, it inspires others to do the same.

63. Original Text:

"မိုးကွမ်းကြားပြီအရပ်"

- *Translation*: "The rain clears, and the ground is visible."

- *Meaning* : Clarity comes after confusion. After a difficult period, things will eventually clear up and become easier to see.

64. Original Text: "အငွေ့မလိုဘဲအရည်"

- *Translation*: "No scent without the liquid."

- **_Meaning_ :** Everything has a cause and effect. You can't expect results without putting in the effort.

65. Original Text:

"ချောင်းတိုင်အပေါ်မှာမရ"

- **_Translation_:** "The river bank cannot stand on its own."

- **_Meaning_ :** It implies that support and collaboration are necessary for survival or success.

66. Original Text: "ရေငံကြီး၏ကျား"

- **_Translation_:** "The crocodile of the great river."

- **_Meaning_ :** This suggests a powerful or significant entity in a large situation—great forces or individuals who have a major impact.

67. Original Text:

"သုသဘီတိလမ်းလျှောက်"

- *Translation*: "The road taken is full of roses."

- *Meaning* : Sometimes, life's challenges and decisions seem difficult, but they lead to beautiful outcomes.

68. Original Text: "အမည်တန်ဖိုးထိုင်နေ"

- *Translation*: "To sit is to earn respect."

- *Meaning* : Inaction, or thoughtful waiting, can often garner respect. Sometimes patience and stillness are more powerful than action.

69. Original Text: "သိုးအိုးတစ်ကြိမ်"

- *Translation*: "One time is enough for the sheep."

- *Meaning* : It speaks to the idea that a single experience can be enough to teach you something valuable.

70. Original Text:

"သတိပြုအောင်လျက်ရှေ့သွား"

- *Translation*: "Move forward, but with caution."

- *Meaning* : Always move towards your goal, but do so carefully and with full awareness of the situation around you.

71. Original Text:

"အရပ်မြေတရားအရာ"

- *Translation*: "The earth itself holds the law."

- *Meaning* : Nature governs life, and everything has its place and purpose in the grand scheme of things.

72. Original Text:

"ထွက်ဝင်သွားသည့်အခါ"

- *Translation*: "When entering, be cautious."

- *Meaning* : This suggests that when entering any situation, be aware of the risks and challenges before proceeding.

73. Original Text: "တံခါးတစ်ပေါက်"

- *Translation*: "The door opens."

- *Meaning* : A new opportunity or possibility is on the horizon. It signifies new beginnings or changes.

74. Original Text: "လမ်းပေါ် ရှိဥ်းတင်"

- *Translation*: "A monkey on the road."

- *Meaning* : It refers to an unexpected or unusual situation, often highlighting the element of surprise in life.

75. Original Text: "အရုပ်တစ်ကောင်ရောက်"

- *Translation*: "One's own doll arrives."

- *Meaning* : This suggests that sometimes what you're looking for will eventually come to you in its own time.

76. Original Text: "ပိလွှေဖောက်သွား"

- *Translation*: "The egg shell cracks."
- *Meaning* : This refers to the idea that a breakthrough is happening. Something new is emerging or being revealed.

77. Original Text: "မြေပြင်မလားပြေး"

- *Translation*: "Don't run without knowing the ground."
- *Meaning* : Don't rush into things without fully understanding the situation. Knowledge and awareness are necessary before making decisions.

78. Original Text: "တံခါးချိတ်ခွဲစီး"

- *Translation*: "The door is open but not wide."

- **_Meaning_ :** Opportunities may be present, but they might be limited. You have to act quickly before the chance closes.

79. Original Text:

"အောက်ဆုံးတင်ကြားမှ"

- **_Translation_:** "The lowest point brings the best lesson."

- **_Meaning_ :** The most difficult or lowest moments often teach us the most valuable lessons.

80. Original Text: "ပျော်ပျော်ဘဝကိုရှင်"

- **_Translation_:** "Live joyfully through life's struggles."

- **_Meaning_ :** Despite difficulties, one should find happiness and joy in life and persevere.

81. Original Text:

"ပုလွေတစ်ကောင်ကြိုဆို"

- **_Translation_:** "A snake welcomes you."

- *Meaning* : A deceptive or dangerous situation may appear welcoming. It advises caution and skepticism.

82. Original Text: "ခွေးသွားပင်လယ်ဆီ"

- *Translation*: "The dog goes to the sea."

- *Meaning* : A person or animal ventures into unfamiliar territory without fully understanding the dangers involved.

83. Original Text: "ကွက်တစ်ခုကြားထွက်"

- *Translation*: "The gap between the fences."

- *Meaning* : There is always an opportunity hidden between the boundaries or limits, and it's about finding that space.

84. Original Text: "ပန်းပင်ကြီးတစ်ကောင်"

- *Translation*: "A giant flower blooms."

- *Meaning* : Great things can come from modest beginnings. It reflects the potential for growth and development.

85. Original Text:
"လှိုင်းစီးတိုင်းမှာတောင်"

- *Translation*: "Even the wave flows to the shore."

- *Meaning* : Life's flow always returns to a beginning or end. It speaks to the cyclical nature of existence.

86. Original Text:
"ကန့်အသတ်လျှောက်ချိန်"

- *Translation*: "The time to cross is limited."

- *Meaning* : Time and opportunities are finite. Act when the time is right before it passes.

87. Original Text:
"စီမံကိန်းအတွက်ရင်းနှီး"

- *Translation*: "To invest is to plan."

- *Meaning* : Investment is not just about money; it's about thought, time, and planning for the future.

88. Original Text: "တင်သွားခဲ့ပြီး"

- *Translation*: "The work was already carried."

- *Meaning* : It speaks to the importance of completing tasks and following through with one's efforts.

89. Original Text:
"တံတားရှုခင်းနောက်ကွယ်"

- *Translation*: "Beyond the bridge, a hidden view."

- *Meaning* : There is always more than meets the eye. We must look beyond the obvious to find greater rewards.

90. Original Text:
"အောင်မြင်သောကောင်းကင်"

- *Translation*: "A successful sky."

- *Meaning* : Success is as vast and limitless as the sky. It speaks to boundless possibilities.

91. Original Text: "သစ်ပင်မြင်ကွင်းမှန်"

- *Translation*: "The tree's view is blocked."

- *Meaning* : Sometimes, we cannot see clearly because of our own distractions or limitations. It's about seeing beyond obstacles.

92. Original Text:
"သင့်တော်သောပြေးခြင်း"

- *Translation*: "Run at your own pace."

- *Meaning* : Do not rush in life; go at the pace that suits you. Everyone's journey is different.

93. Original Text: "သပိတ်လှိုင်အသွား"

- *Translation*: "The bullock cart takes the load."

- *Meaning* : Hard work and effort lead to carrying burdens, but they eventually bring results or success.

94. Original Text: "သစ်ပင်အရောက်ကပ်"

- *Translation*: "The tree stands against the wind."

- *Meaning* : Resilience in the face of adversity. No matter how difficult things get, you must stand strong.

95. Original Text: "ဆွတ်မြေလမ်းမှရှည်"

- *Translation*: "The road stretches beyond the hill."

- *Meaning* : There's always more to explore, and life's journey never ends. New opportunities always await beyond current horizons.

96. Original Text: "မြင့်မားသောသရဖူ"

- *Translation*: "The highest peak calls."

- *Meaning* : Challenges at the highest level demand your attention, representing the pursuit of greatness.

97. Original Text: "လှည့်တယ်ဆိုတဲ့တောင်"

- *Translation*: "Even the mountain spins."

- *Meaning* : No matter how steady something seems, everything is subject to change or movement.

98. Original Text: "ထိုင်ခုံအထက်တင်"

- *Translation*: "The chair sits above the rest."

- *Meaning* : The position of authority or leadership is earned and represents responsibility.

99. Original Text:

"မြေမှာမြတ်သောကြောင်"

- *Translation*: "A cat that respects the earth."

- *Meaning* : Being grounded and humble in life is crucial. Even those who seem self-sufficient should maintain humility.

100. Original Text:

"လောကကြီးအတိုင်းအတာ"

- *Translation*: "The vastness of the world."

- *Meaning* : Life is vast, and every decision or action you take impacts the world in ways you may not fully understand.

101. Original Text:

"သောက်တယ်ဆိုရင်ကြက်သေ"

- *Translation*: "Drinking leads to chicken death."

- **_Meaning_ :** Overindulgence can lead to negative consequences, reminding us to practice moderation.

102. **Original Text:**
"ပြောင်းရွှေ့တဲ့လမ်းကိုရွေး"

- **_Translation_:** "Choose the road that leads to change."

- **_Meaning_ :** Embrace change as a path for growth and progress in life.

103. **Original Text:**
"ဘုရားစောင့်လမ်း"

- **_Translation_:** "The path guarded by the god."

- **_Meaning_ :** There's protection in following the right path, suggesting divine guidance and security.

104. **Original Text:**
"မြေပြင်ငယ်တစ်ခု"

- **_Translation_**: "A small piece of land."

- **_Meaning_** : This refers to humble beginnings and making the most of small opportunities.

105. Original Text: "လက်ပတ်ပြင်လှာအောင်"

- **_Translation_**: "The wrist adornment shines brightly."

- **_Meaning_** : This signifies that beauty or value is often in the details and how you carry yourself.

106. Original Text: "မိုးလုံလေလုံကွင်း"

- **_Translation_**: "The storm and the gentle breeze meet."

- **_Meaning_** : Life contains both hardships and calm moments. It suggests that balance exists in all situations.

107. Original Text:
"လက်မောင်းတော်ဝင်"

- *Translation*: "The sleeve hides the secret."

- *Meaning* : Some things are hidden from view, and not everything is as it seems. Secrets or hidden aspects exist beneath the surface.

108. Original Text:
"သွားတစ်ဆင့်လမ်း"

- *Translation*: "One step at a time."

- *Meaning* : Progress is made slowly, and patience and persistence are key to achieving long-term goals.

109. Original Text:
"လျှောင့်ပြင်းတပ်တံ"

- *Translation*: "A sharp turn at the end."

- ***Meaning*** : Life has unexpected turns, and one must be ready to adapt when the time comes.

110. **110.   Original Text:**
"ထိုးစီးခိုင်းသောတံတား"

- ***Translation***: "The bridge withstands the weight."

- ***Meaning*** : Strong foundations and preparations help withstand challenges and difficulties.

111.   **Original Text:**
"ဆွေဖေါ်ပွားစောင်"

- ***Translation***: "The branch blooms with blossoms."

- ***Meaning*** : Hard work and nurture lead to positive outcomes, representing growth and achievement.

112.   **Original Text:**
"တစ်ခါသင်မေးလေ့ရှိ"

- **_Translation_**: "You once asked for help."

- **_Meaning_** : Don't forget the help you received in the past when it's your turn to give.

113. Original Text: "စစ်ပွဲအပြီးမှ"

- **_Translation_**: "After the battle is over."

- **_Meaning_** : This signifies that peace and resolution come only after overcoming struggles or conflicts.

114. Original Text: "ကလေးခြေတော်မှထွက်"

- **_Translation_**: "The child walks from the front."

- **_Meaning_** : New generations or fresh ideas lead the way forward.

115. Original Text: "သင်တန်းကတင်သွား"

- *Translation*: "The lecture will be delivered."

- *Meaning* : Wisdom or knowledge will be passed on. It refers to the sharing of experience and learning.

116. Original Text: "အရက်လောက်ပေါ်တွင်မှ"

- *Translation*: "From the tip of the bottle."

- *Meaning* : The start of something small can lead to bigger consequences, often used as a cautionary statement about moderation.

117. Original Text: "ရွှေလျားသောငါး"

- *Translation*: "The fish on the move."

- *Meaning* : This symbolizes that progress is constant, and we must adapt to changes as they come.

118. Original Text:
"လျှပ်စစ်နှင့်မဂ်လာ"

- *Translation*: "Electricity with luck."

- *Meaning* : Even when the resources or circumstances are ready, luck plays a vital role in success.

119. Original Text:
"မျက်နှာဘက်ကွယ်"

- *Translation*: "Hidden behind the face."

- *Meaning* : What is visible on the outside may hide deeper emotions or thoughts.

120. Original Text:
"လမ်းအတိုင်းမစီး"

- *Translation*: "Do not travel the road as is."

- *Meaning* : Challenges may arise if one follows a path without considering the obstacles ahead, and one must plan ahead.

121. Original Text:
"ရွှေရည်တစ်ခုပို့"

- *Translation*: "A golden drop falls."

- *Meaning* : It refers to a valuable or rare opportunity that may arise unexpectedly.

122. Original Text:
"လေထုအမြဲတမ်း"

- *Translation*: "The wind is constant."

- *Meaning* : It emphasizes the inevitability of change or forces beyond control.

123. Original Text:
"တိုးတက်မှုအမြင့်"

- *Translation*: "The peak of progress."

- **Meaning** : Reaching the highest point of success or achievement through consistent hard work.

124. Original Text: "မြေကိုရှာနေ"

- **Translation**: "Searching the ground."

- **Meaning** : Represents a journey to discover something important or valuable, searching for deeper Meaning or resources.

125. Original Text: "ရင်ပြင်စွပ်တည်"

- **Translation**: "The heart is steady."

- **Meaning** : Remaining calm and composed in the face of adversity or challenges.

126. Original Text: "မြင်တွေ့ရခက်သေး"

- **Translation**: "It's hard to see clearly."

- *Meaning* : Sometimes clarity takes time, and one must remain patient to understand the bigger picture.

127. Original Text:
"ဆင်တစ်ကောင်လိုက်"

- *Translation*: "The elephant follows."

- *Meaning* : A symbol of persistence and strength, it suggests that slow and steady progress will eventually lead to success.

128. Original Text:
"သစ်သားလျှောက်သူ"

- *Translation*: "One who treads on new wood."

- *Meaning* : It refers to those who venture into new beginnings, paths, or unfamiliar situations.

129. Original Text:
"ပိတောက်များလေး"

- **_Translation_**: "The chameleon changes its colors."

- **_Meaning_** : Adaptability is necessary to survive in varying conditions or situations.

130. Original Text:
"နန်းပေါ်ရောက်လား"

- **_Translation_**: "Reaching the throne."

- **_Meaning_** : Achieving the highest position or goal after much struggle and perseverance.

131. Original Text:
"ခေါင်းငယ်ကတည်လမ်း"

- **_Translation_**: "The small head leads the way."

- **_Meaning_** : Sometimes, new or smaller perspectives offer the best solutions. Innovation often comes from unexpected sources.

132. Original Text:
"အပြုံးလေးခရား"

- *Translation*: "A smile hides the secret."

- *Meaning* : People may hide their true feelings or intentions behind a smile, suggesting not everything is as it appears.

133. Original Text:
"လေပြေလမ်းညွှန်"

- *Translation*: "The wind guides the way."

- *Meaning* : Sometimes, the right path is found by following natural forces or intuition.

134. Original Text:
"ချစ်ခြင်းမေတ္တာကိုဖောက်"

- *Translation*: "The love will break."

- *Meaning* : Love, like any strong emotion, can be fragile. It warns about taking love for granted.

135.   Original Text:

"ခရီးတစ်ခုလိုက်ပါ"

- *Translation*: "Follow the path."

- *Meaning* : Life's journey should be undertaken with purpose and direction, moving toward a set goal.

136.   Original Text:

"ခင်မင်တတ်သောသူ"

- *Translation*: "The one who knows how to love."

- *Meaning* : True wisdom lies in the ability to love and care for others, showing the importance of compassion.

137.   Original Text:

"ကိုယ်တိုင်ပျော်ကြ"

- *Translation*: "Happiness is within oneself."

- **_Meaning_ :** True happiness comes from within, not from external sources.

138.   Original Text: "ဆက်လက်သွားလိမ့်မယ်"

- **_Translation_:** "Keep going forward."

- **_Meaning_ :** Perseverance is key in any endeavor. No matter how hard the journey, continuing to move forward is essential.

139.   Original Text: "လမ်းမပျက်"

- **_Translation_:** "The road never fails."

- **_Meaning_ :** With persistence and steady effort, the path will eventually lead to success.

140.   Original Text: "မှတ်မိသည့်မိုး"

- **_Translation_:** "The remembered rain."

- **_Meaning_ :** Things from the past can bring valuable lessons or nostalgia that influence current decisions.

141.   Original Text:
"တောတောင်မြင့်တယ်"

- **_Translation_:** "The mountain grows taller."

- **_Meaning_ :** Growth is continuous, and progress can always be made despite challenges.

142.   Original Text:
"မျက်လုံးမပိတ်"

- **_Translation_:** "Eyes never close."

- **_Meaning_ :** The truth always finds a way to be seen. One can never hide the truth forever.

143.   Original Text:
"နောက်သို့ပြန်မရ"

- **_Translation_:** "There's no turning back."

- _**Meaning**_ : Once a decision is made, you must face the consequences and move forward without regret.

144.   Original Text:
"သတိထားဖို့လမ်း"

- _**Translation**_: "The road needs caution."

- _**Meaning**_ : Life's journey requires careful consideration and mindfulness to avoid mistakes or dangers.

145.   Original Text:
"ပေါက်မည့်ရေငယ်"

- _**Translation**_: "The breaking water flows."

- _**Meaning**_ : Once a barrier is broken, everything moves forward with greater momentum. It represents overcoming obstacles.

146. Original Text:

"ရုပ်တစ်ပုံနဲ့မလွဲ"

- **_Translation_**: "No mistake with the right image."

- **_Meaning_** : When clarity and truth are clear, there's no room for error or misunderstanding.

147. Original Text:

"ကွင်းတစ်ခုမှထွက်"

- **_Translation_**: "Step out of the circle."

- **_Meaning_** : Sometimes, stepping outside your comfort zone is necessary to gain a new perspective or opportunity.

148. Original Text:

"သနပ်ခါးသေးစွာ"

- **_Translation_**: "Even the smallest effort counts."

- *Meaning* : Every little effort or contribution matters, no matter how insignificant it may seem.

"ပင်လယ်စွန်းသည်ငါး"

- *Translation*: "The shore receives the fish."

- *Meaning* : It suggests that opportunities will eventually come to those who are patient and wait for the right time.

"ပြန်လည်ရောက်ရှိတယ်"

- *Translation*: "The return is inevitable."

- *Meaning* : What goes around comes around; actions and consequences are often cyclical.

"ဆင်တစ်ကောင်ဖြစ်တယ်"

- ***Translation***: "The elephant is created."

- ***Meaning*** : A grand creation or achievement, signifying hard work and effort have led to something substantial.

152. Original Text:
"လွယ်ကူမှုမျိုးကောင်း"

- ***Translation***: "Ease brings goodness."

- ***Meaning*** : Sometimes the easiest path leads to the best outcome, as things fall into place effortlessly.

153. Original Text:
"ကွယ်ဝှက်မှုများ"

- ***Translation***: "Hidden things."

- ***Meaning*** : Secrets or hidden truths always exist beneath the surface, reminding us that not everything is visible.

154.   Original Text:
"စံအတွက်မြေခြစ်"

- *Translation*: "The land is dug for the stake."

- *Meaning* : It suggests that effort and work must be put in before achieving any major result.

155.   Original Text:
"လောင်စစ်စင်ပါ"

- *Translation*: "The fire burns clean."

- *Meaning* : A pure force or intention will always lead to a positive outcome, free from corruption.

156.   Original Text:
"မြစ်ပေါ်မှာလှီး"

- *Translation*: "The boat on the river."

- *Meaning* : You are like a boat on the river of life, constantly moving forward with purpose and direction.

Original Text:
"ဘုရားသခင်စိမ်းစွပ်"

- **_Translation_**: "The god wears new robes."

- **_Meaning_** : New beginnings, or the divine preparing for something fresh and great.

158. **Original Text:**
"ပြားဖြတ်စီးဆင်း"

- **_Translation_**: "Cut through the bread."

- **_Meaning_** : It signifies decisive action or cutting through obstacles with determination.

159. **Original Text:**
"ညီညာသွားသ"

- **_Translation_**: "The one who goes straight."

- **_Meaning_ :** It emphasizes staying true to one's path, following a clear and direct route without deviation.

160. **Original Text:**
"ကြောင်ကတစ်မျက်နှာ"

- **_Translation_:** "The cat looks at its reflection."

- **_Meaning_ :** It symbolizes self-awareness, introspection, or recognizing oneself in various situations.

161. **Original Text:**
"ရေတိမ်တစ်စီး"

- **_Translation_:** "A boat on the water."

- **_Meaning_ :** This signifies a peaceful journey or the need to be adaptable to life's flow and changes.

162.   Original Text:
"အပင်ထွက်သည့်ရင်"

- **_Translation_**: "The branch that grows."

- **_Meaning_** : Growth is inevitable when the right conditions are met, symbolizing potential and development.

163.   Original Text:
"ကမ်းခြေကိုပြေး"

- **_Translation_**: "Run to the shore."

- **_Meaning_** : Seek refuge or security when the storm or challenge becomes too great.

164.   Original Text:
"အမှတ်တရခင်းစရာ"

- **_Translation_**: "A memory is carved."

- **_Meaning_** : Moments in life are engraved in our memories, and these memories shape who we are.

"သဘော်တင်ထားသည်"

- *Translation*: "The boat is anchored."

- *Meaning* : Rest or taking a pause is necessary before continuing on the journey.

"ခေါင်လုံးမေ့ကြ"

- *Translation*: "The sky does not forget."

- *Meaning* : Nature or the universe keeps track of everything, and nothing escapes its attention.

"တစ်ထွက်တစ်ပြန်"

- *Translation*: "One step leads to another."

- *Meaning* : Small actions lead to bigger opportunities; progress is made one step at a time.

"တရားစွပ်ပြုံး"

- *Translation*: "Truth wears a smile."

- *Meaning* : The truth is often more approachable or gentle than we expect, and it eventually reveals itself.

"လေထုချင်းခိုင်"

- *Translation*: "The wind never forgets."

- *Meaning* : Similar to nature, our actions have lasting consequences, and time will reveal the effects.

"တောင်တက်ပေါက်လျှော"

- *Translation*: "Climb the mountain to cross the river."

- _Meaning_ : It's often necessary to overcome great challenges before reaching the solution or reward.

171.   **Original Text:**
"မနက်ခင်းမှာတိုးတက်"

- _Translation_: "The morning rises with growth."

- _Meaning_ : A new beginning, full of potential for progress and change, every new day holds the chance to improve.

172.   **Original Text:**
"သုံးထပ်မြေအောက်"

- _Translation_: "The land beneath the three layers."

- _Meaning_ : Things are often more complex than they appear; there are hidden depths beneath what we see.

173.   **Original Text:**
"သင်ခန်းစာတစ်ခုကွယ်"

- *Translation*: "A lesson is hidden."

- *Meaning* : There is wisdom or knowledge embedded in every experience, even if it's not immediately apparent.

174.   Original Text: "တစ်လှည့်တိုက်ဆွဲ"

- *Translation*: "The turn brings you forward."

- *Meaning* : Every twist and turn in life leads you to new possibilities and growth.

175.   Original Text: "သုတ်ခတ်ကိုဖော်ထုတ်"

- *Translation*: "The brush uncovers the truth."

- *Meaning* : The act of revealing or cleaning up can uncover hidden truths, much like clearing away dust to see clearly.

176. Original Text:

"အောင်မြင်မှုတစ်လှည့်"

- *Translation*: "Success in every turn."

- *Meaning* : Every effort or attempt leads toward success. Small victories accumulate to create bigger triumphs.

177. Original Text:

"နတ်တရားမျှတ"

- *Translation*: "God's justice is fair."

- *Meaning* : The higher power or universe distributes fairness in the end, even if it seems delayed.

178. Original Text:

"ဘောပင်စည်းမမှား"

- *Translation*: "The rope does not fail."

- *Meaning* : Trustworthy and dependable, like a solid and

unbreakable connection that guides you.

179. **Original Text:** "တုန်လှန်ဖို့လမ်း"

- ***Translation***: "The road leads to retreat."
- ***Meaning*** **:** Sometimes, stepping back is necessary to gain a better perspective or to plan a better approach.

180. **Original Text:** "ခိုင်မာတဲ့ထိပ်တံ"

- ***Translation***: "The sturdy top of the mountain."
- ***Meaning*** **:** The best results or most reliable outcomes come from a solid foundation.

181. **Original Text:** "ထောင်ပါဘယ်လိုကြို"

- ***Translation***: "How to deal with the mountain."

- *Meaning* : The way to handle a difficult task or challenge depends on how you approach it.

Original Text:
"ငါးရေကိုအတု"

- *Translation*: "The fish follows the current."

- *Meaning* : Following the natural flow can sometimes lead to success, especially when you go with the flow of life.

Original Text:
"စက်ဘီးရှိနဲ့ပ"

- *Translation*: "Press the bicycle pedal."

- *Meaning* : Small, continuous actions lead to progress and eventual achievement.

Original Text:
"အိုးဖွားခေါင်းတောင်"

- **_Translation_:** "Even the pot has a lid."

- **_Meaning_ :** Every problem or challenge has a solution, just as every vessel has a cover.

185. Original Text:

"မှုဆိုးများတက်"

- **_Translation_:** "The owls rise."

- **_Meaning_ :** When the time is right, wisdom or knowledge will appear, even from unexpected sources.

186. Original Text:

"အသက်ရှင်စိတ်များ"

- **_Translation_:** "The living spirits are abundant."

- **_Meaning_ :** Life is full of vitality and potential, and there is a deep force behind all living things.

187. Original Text:

"ပန်းကန်ထဲသို့ရွှေး"

- *Translation*: "Choose the plate."

- *Meaning* : In situations of choice, one must make a decision or select a path, even when there are multiple options.

188. Original Text: "လက်ချို့ငွေကြီး"

- *Translation*: "Big wealth in your hands."

- *Meaning* : Opportunities for success and prosperity often come into our hands, but we must be prepared to grasp them.

189. Original Text: "ကြက်နှာဖွဲတင်း"

- *Translation*: "The chicken's wing rises."

- *Meaning* : Even a small action or gesture can have significant impact if done with purpose.

190. Original Text:
"မြေထဲမှလေး"

- **_Translation_**: "The four from the earth."

- **_Meaning_** : Refers to the four corners of the earth, symbolizing the vastness and unpredictability of the world.

191. Original Text:
"အဝတ်လေးယင်"

- **_Translation_**: "The light robe."

- **_Meaning_** : This suggests simplicity and grace, indicating that elegance often comes from modest means.

192. Original Text:
"နှင်းကျော်လမ်း"

- **_Translation_**: "The road through the snow."

- **_Meaning_** : It represents overcoming obstacles to reach your destination, even when conditions are harsh.

193. Original Text: "ဖောင်းဆိုးရိုက်တယ်"

- *Translation*: "The smoke rises high."

- *Meaning* : Sometimes, actions create noticeable consequences, or people's efforts draw attention.

194. Original Text: "ချွတ်တယ်ဆိုလျှင်အောင်"

- *Translation*: "Success comes after overcoming the fall."

- *Meaning* : Failure is not the end; rather, it is a step toward eventual success when you rise again.

195. Original Text: "ခွက်မတွေ့နာ"

- *Translation*: "The bowl never overflows."

- **_Meaning_ :** A situation has limits, and it teaches us to be mindful of our capacity or resources.

196.   Original Text:
"ထင်ရှားသောပုလင်း"

- **_Translation_:** "The visible bottle."

- **_Meaning_ :** Things that are apparent or obvious are often easy to address, unlike hidden challenges.

197.   Original Text:
"လုံလောက်တဲ့လေဖြတ်"

- **_Translation_:** "Sufficient wind to sail."

- **_Meaning_ :** When the conditions are right, success becomes inevitable. It's all about timing.

198.   Original Text:
"ခရီးကိုညွှန်ကြား"

- **_Translation_:** "Guide the journey."

- _**Meaning**_ : It's essential to provide direction in life, just like a guide helps a traveler on an unknown path.

199. Original Text: "အာဏာရှိတဲ့လမ်း"

- _**Translation**_: "The road with power."

- _**Meaning**_ : Power comes from the right path, and those who walk with purpose often wield influence.

200. Original Text: "လယ်သမားကြိုးကိုခြင်"

- _**Translation**_: "The farmer ties the rope."

- _**Meaning**_ : Every task, no matter how small, needs effort and focus for success.

201. Original Text: "နေရာမှာကြီးမား"

- *Translation*: "Grow in your place."
- *Meaning* : One must thrive in the environment they are in, focusing on their own growth and contribution.

202. **Original Text:** "အတွင်းကတန်း"

- *Translation*: "The internal line."
- *Meaning* : True strength comes from within. Focus on inner qualities to guide external actions.

203. **Original Text:** "အလွန်အမင်းကူး"

- *Translation*: "To cross the ultimate limit."
- *Meaning* : Pushing past all barriers or limits leads to success and achievement.

204. **Original Text:** "ကလေးသစ်တော"

- *Translation*: "The forest of new trees."
- *Meaning* : A new generation or fresh start brings hope and renewal to the future.

205. Original Text: "ပန်းတော်သန့်"

- *Translation*: "The flower is clean."
- *Meaning* : Purity and beauty are found in simplicity and integrity, representing clarity of intention.

206. Original Text: "အရက်မရောင်း"

- *Translation*: "Do not sell alcohol."
- *Meaning* : The proverb warns against selling something that can cause harm or lead others astray.

207. Original Text: "အဝတ်မြှောက်တင်"

- *Translation*: "Raise the clothes."

- *Meaning* : Elevate your efforts or status with dignity, keeping your integrity intact.

208. Original Text: "ကောင်းစွာရှောင်ကာ"

- *Translation*: "Avoid well."

- *Meaning* : Avoiding unnecessary conflicts or danger leads to peace and success.

209. Original Text: "ပြင်းထန်သောအရောင်"

- *Translation*: "The intense color."

- *Meaning* : Strong emotions or actions often leave a deep impression or impact.

210. Original Text: "အောင်မြင်ရသောသူ"

- *Translation*: "The one who succeeds."

- **_Meaning_ :** Success comes to those who persist and remain focused on their goals.

211. Original Text: "စွန့်လွတ်မှုတိုင်း"

- **_Translation_:** "Every freedom comes with a cost."

- **_Meaning_ :** Freedom or success often requires sacrifices, and nothing comes without effort.

212. Original Text: "ဘဲရောက်လျှင်ရှာ"

- **_Translation_:** "Seek when the hen arrives."

- **_Meaning_ :** Opportunities should be seized when they arise, as they may not come again.

213. Original Text: "ချွတ်ခြင်းကမ်းလှမ်း"

- **_Translation_:** "The invitation to cross."

- *Meaning* : Sometimes, challenges are opportunities disguised as obstacles, inviting one to grow beyond limits.

214. Original Text: "လှည်းမထွက်သောအဖေ"

- *Translation*: "The father who never left the cart."

- *Meaning* : This suggests that staying committed and not abandoning responsibilities is key to long-term success.

215. Original Text: "ဓမ္မနှင့်ကိုင်တား"

- *Translation*: "Hold the law with care."

- *Meaning* : It's important to uphold justice or integrity, but with wisdom and mindfulness.

216. Original Text: "မှဆိုးလွတ်မြှောက်"

- *Translation*: "The owl escapes."

- *Meaning* : A clever or wise person can often find a way out of tricky situations or dangers.

217. Original Text:
"ပို့ကြွားသောပင်လယ်"

- *Translation*: "The bride's ocean."

- *Meaning* : Life can be filled with challenges, but through persistence, one can find peace.

218. Original Text: "နတ်ရဲ့အမြင်"

- *Translation*: "The god's sight."

- *Meaning* : The higher perspective reveals the broader picture, where human limitations are overcome.

219. Original Text:
"ကြီးကျယ်သောမြေ"

- *Translation*: "The vast land."

- *Meaning* : Life offers endless possibilities, and opportunities are abundant for those willing to search.

220. Original Text: "ရော့မကျွံသောလေ"

- **Translation**: "The wind that doesn't fade."

- **Meaning** : Steadfastness and persistence are qualities that allow one to endure challenges without losing momentum.

221. Original Text: "နွားရဲ့တီ"

- **Translation**: "The cow's calf."

- **Meaning** : Sometimes, efforts take time to mature and bear fruit. Patience is necessary for growth.

222. Original Text: "အခြားဓမ္မတရား"

- **Translation**: "Other's law is sacred."

- *Meaning* : Respect the boundaries and rules set by others, as we all share the same space in life.

"ဘုရားအဘို့သန့်"

- *Translation*: "Purity for the god."

- *Meaning* : Offering one's best and purest effort or thoughts to a greater cause.

"မောင်းတာဖြင့်ပျော်"

- *Translation*: "Find joy in driving."

- *Meaning* : In every task or effort, the enjoyment comes not from the destination but from the process itself.

"ဖက်တော်ရဲ့လှုပ်ရှား"

- *Translation*: "The movement of the balance."

- **_Meaning_ :** Life's equilibrium must be maintained, and even small shifts can have great effects.

226. **Original Text:**
"ဝတ်ဖုံးနှင့်မနိုး"

- **_Translation_:** "Do not rise with the blanket."

- **_Meaning_ :** In times of challenge, it is important to rise early and face adversity, not to stay complacent.

227. **Original Text:**
"ယောဂလမ်းတည်"

- **_Translation_:** "The yoga path is steady."

- **_Meaning_ :** Achieving balance and peace in life requires regular practice and self-discipline.

228. **Original Text:** "ငါ့ကိုကိုင်ပါ"

- **_Translation_:** "Hold me."

- _**Meaning**_ : This signifies the importance of support from others during difficult times.

229. **Original Text:** "ကြီးခဲမက်အတ္တာ"

- _**Translation**_: "The thick clothes of the elephant."

- _**Meaning**_ : Toughness or resilience is built over time and with repeated experiences.

230. **Original Text:** "အမိန့်ရှိန်မှ ကြိုး"

- _**Translation**_: "The rope of the command."

- _**Meaning**_ : Power or control comes from one's ability to bind or unify forces under a single directive.

231. **Original Text:** "မြေနေ့ရောက်"

- _**Translation**_: "The land arrives at the day."

- **_Meaning_ :** Things fall into place at the right moment, and everything will happen when the time is right.

232. Original Text:
"တော်တော်ကောင်းကောင်း"

- **_Translation_:** "Good, very good."

- **_Meaning_ :** A positive outcome or result, when things go exceptionally well.

233. Original Text:
"ဝတ်နယ်တံခါး"

- **_Translation_:** "The door to wear the cloth."

- **_Meaning_ :** Even minor things need care and attention in order to proceed effectively.

234. Original Text:
"နွားကေးတော်"

- **_Translation_:** "The cow gives more."

- *Meaning* : Those who have the most to give often share it generously, showing abundance and goodwill.

235.   **Original Text:**
"လျှပ်စစ်မီးအိုး"

- *Translation*: "Electric stove."

- *Meaning* : New technology or innovation leads to faster, more efficient ways of doing things.

236.   **Original Text:**
"စွယ်စုံစံအလင်း"

- *Translation*: "The light of the full moon."

- *Meaning* : Clarity or truth is often revealed when things are most illuminated.

237.   **Original Text:**
"ပင်လယ်စွမ်းအား"

- *Translation*: "The power of the ocean."

- *Meaning* : Nature or unseen forces can have immense power, and we must be respectful of their strength.

238. Original Text:
"သစ်ပင်ရွှေပင်"

- *Translation*: "The gold tree."

- *Meaning* : A symbol of prosperity and value, representing things or people with high worth.

239. Original Text:
"ညဉ့်ပွင့်တော်"

- *Translation*: "The flower blooms at night."

- *Meaning* : Beauty or success can sometimes emerge in unexpected or less obvious times.

240. Original Text:
"အမြင်တစ်မျိုးသာ"

- *Translation*: "One perspective only."

- **_Meaning_ :** It reminds us that seeing things from a single viewpoint can limit understanding; multiple perspectives are needed.

241.   Original Text:
"ပင်လယ်မိုးသစ်"

- **_Translation_:** "The ocean's new rain."

- **_Meaning_ :** New beginnings or refreshing changes that bring life and renewal.

242.   Original Text:
"ရောဂါထဲမှဖြတ်"

- **_Translation_:** "Cross through illness."

- **_Meaning_ :** Overcoming hardship and challenges leads to personal growth and strength.

243.   Original Text:
"ဘီလပ်ရဲ့တိုးတက်မှု"

- **_Translation_**: "The advancement of the stone."

- **_Meaning_** : Even things that seem immovable or slow to change can progress with time and effort.

"ကိုယ်တိုင်ပင်တိုးတက်"

- **_Translation_**: "Self-growth."

- **_Meaning_** : The best growth comes from within, and personal development is the most valuable kind of progress.

"အလျားအရှည်စွမ်း"

- **_Translation_**: "Endless power."

- **_Meaning_** : True strength and resilience come from an unyielding force or effort that never runs out.

"ထွန်းလင်းသောစေတီ"

- *Translation*: "The shining stupa."

- *Meaning* : A symbol of spiritual illumination, wisdom, and clarity that guides one's life.

247.   **Original Text:** "ကလေးနောက်တရား"

- *Translation*: "The child's rear path."

- *Meaning* : Sometimes, the most fruitful results come from unexpected or indirect routes.

248.   **Original Text:** "ပင်လယ်ကြီးသောမြစ်"

- *Translation*: "The river of the great ocean."

- *Meaning* : Large forces of nature, or overwhelming situations, are difficult to navigate but can be dealt with by persistence.

249.   **Original Text:** "ခွေးကိုဖိတ်ခေါ်"

- **_Translation_:** "Call the dog."

- **_Meaning_ :** A warning against inviting trouble or unnecessary challenges into your life.

250. Original Text: "နှိပ်ငြိမ်းလေးမောက်"

- **_Translation_:** "To calm the storm."

- **_Meaning_ :** Peace and calmness come with patience and understanding, even in turbulent situations.

251. Original Text: "ပုံပြင်မှမှတ်တမ်း"

- **_Translation_:** "From story to record."

- **_Meaning_ :** What is once a story becomes a memory or historical record, emphasizing the power of storytelling.

252. Original Text: "ငါ့ကိုမျှော်လင့်"

- *Translation*: "Expect from me."

- *Meaning* : The expectations set by others can lead to either fulfillment or disappointment, depending on how one meets them.

253. Original Text:
"နှစ်ချို့မော်လုံး"

- *Translation*: "The two rings are joined."

- *Meaning* : Unity is powerful; when two forces combine, they create a stronger bond.

254. Original Text:
"သတိထားလမ်းပြည့်"

- *Translation*: "Be cautious on the full road."

- *Meaning* : Be careful and aware, especially when you are on a path that is long and full of potential dangers.

255. **Original Text:**

"ဘေးရဲ့အကူအညီ"

- *Translation*: "Help from the side."
- *Meaning*: Sometimes support comes from unexpected places, often from those who are not in the center of the action.

256. **Original Text:**

"ကံကောင်းသောကျွဲ"

- *Translation*: "The lucky buffalo."
- *Meaning*: Luck sometimes favors the most unlikely of beings, proving that fortune is unpredictable.

257. **Original Text:**

"လယ်ပင်တစ်ခုကိုရောက်"

- *Translation*: "Reach the farm's edge."
- *Meaning*: Reaching the final stage of any endeavor is a rewarding and fulfilling achievement.

258.   **Original Text:**
"အစားအစာမညီ"

- *Translation*: "The food doesn't match."

- *Meaning* : This refers to things that are incompatible or mismatched, signaling a need for better alignment.

259.   **Original Text:**
"ထထဲသောမိုး"

- *Translation*: "The thick cloud."

- *Meaning* : Dark times or confusion will eventually clear, as the clouds of difficulty are transient.

260.   **Original Text:**
"စိတ်သွားသွားပြန်ပြန်"

- *Translation*: "The mind wanders back and forth."

- *Meaning* : This speaks to the restlessness of the mind, and the importance of focus in achieving one's goals.

261. Original Text:
"ငါးနက်စွန်းစီး"

- **Translation:** "The fish swims in the dark."

- **Meaning :** Sometimes, one must navigate through unknown or challenging circumstances to find success.

262. Original Text:
"ရေတံတစ်ခုဖွင့်"

- **Translation:** "Open the dam."

- **Meaning :** A powerful or overwhelming force, once released, can lead to great change.

263. Original Text:
"အတောကပွတ်တတ်"

- **Translation:** "The animal is ready to leap."

- *Meaning* : When a situation is ripe for action, one must be ready to take the opportunity without hesitation.

264. Original Text:
"တောင်ကြီးကျွေးမန်"

- *Translation*: "The mountain nurtures the valley."

- *Meaning* : One's success or growth is often influenced by their environment or support systems.

265. Original Text:
"စကားနည်းသူ"

- *Translation*: "The person of few words."

- *Meaning* : Sometimes silence speaks louder than words, and a person of few words can carry more weight in their actions.

266. Original Text:
"ကွင်းပတ်မှာနတ်"

- **_Translation_**: "The god in the circle."

- **_Meaning_** : Life is cyclical, and all things eventually return to their origins, often with a new perspective.

267. Original Text:
"ရိုးရှင်းသောမြေ"

- **_Translation_**: "The simple earth."

- **_Meaning_** : Simplicity often holds the greatest value, as complexity can obscure what is truly important.

268. Original Text:
"ငွေသားရောင်းပြီးအိုး"

- **_Translation_**: "Sell gold to buy a pot."

- **_Meaning_** : Sacrificing something valuable for a short-term gain may not be a wise decision in the long term.

269. Original Text:
"မြင်းတစ်ကောင်လမ်း"

- *Translation*: "The horse leads the path."

- *Meaning* : Leadership and guidance often come from the front, where one must pave the way for others.

270. Original Text:
"ပုလင်းအများနှင့်"

- *Translation*: "The bottles are many."

- *Meaning* : Options are abundant in life; sometimes it's difficult to choose the right one.

271. Original Text:
"လေကြီးရဲ့တံခါး"

- *Translation*: "The wind's door."

- *Meaning* : Opportunities or changes can come unexpectedly, and it's essential to be prepared when they do.

"အမြဲတမ်းခင်းစရာ"

- *Translation*: "The constant need for care."

- *Meaning* : Certain things in life require continuous attention and nurturing for long-term success.

"ပြန်လည်ဖုံးထား"

- *Translation*: "Cover it back."

- *Meaning* : It's important to resolve or cover up things that may have been left undone or incomplete.

"ကြက်တောင်ပြုတ်အောင်"

- *Translation*: "The rooster crowed to the mountain."

- **_Meaning_ :** No matter how loud or enthusiastic one may be, nature will remain unaffected by human noise.

275.   Original Text:
"အလှုမပြတ်ရွှေ"

- **_Translation_:** "Endlessly shining gold."

- **_Meaning_ :** Beauty or value is constant and does not fade with time.

276.   Original Text:
"အနောက်တံခါးသို့"

- **_Translation_:** "The back door leads."

- **_Meaning_ :** Sometimes, the best opportunities or solutions lie in unexpected or hidden places.

277.   Original Text:
"ကျောကုလားသတိ"

- **_Translation_:** "Mind your back."

- *Meaning* : Always be aware of those around you and be cautious of hidden threats or challenges.

278. **Original Text:**
"နေရောင်မရှိသောလေ"

- *Translation*: "The wind without sunlight."

- *Meaning* : A situation lacking clarity or warmth, leading to confusion or a lack of direction.

279. **Original Text:**
"သက်သေစွမ်းအား"

- *Translation*: "The strength of evidence."

- *Meaning* : Actions speak louder than words, and solid proof brings credibility and support.

280. **Original Text:**
"တောင်ခြေကျက်ပြား"

- *Translation*: "The mountain's edge."

- *Meaning* : Reaching the brink or the boundary of a challenge requires courage and determination.

281. **Original Text:**
"လှည်းမက်ထားသောစေတီ"

- *Translation*: "The stupa with no cart."

- *Meaning* : Something lacking the support it needs may not fulfill its purpose or potential.

282. **Original Text:**
"သင်စွဲမထားသောထိုင်"

- *Translation*: "The seat you didn't hold."

- *Meaning* : Sometimes opportunities slip away because we fail to act at the right moment.

283. **Original Text:**
"စိတ်အားထက်သန်"

- *Translation*: "A spirited mind."

- **_Meaning_ :** The mind is a powerful force, and enthusiasm or passion can fuel progress.

284.   Original Text:
"ချုပ်လှမ်းချက်"

- **_Translation_:** "The closing gesture."

- **_Meaning_ :** Every action, decision, or journey must come to an end eventually.

285.   Original Text:
"မျက်လုံးအမြင့်"

- **_Translation_:** "Eyes on the height."

- **_Meaning_ :** Always aim high, and set your sights on greater aspirations.

286.   Original Text:
"တည်ရှိသောကြောင့်"

- **_Translation_:** "Because it exists."

- *Meaning* : There's purpose and *Meaning* in existence itself, and everything happens for a reason.

287. Original Text:
"စွမ်းအားတိမ်"

- *Translation*: "The fog of power."

- *Meaning* : Power can often be unclear or misunderstood, making it difficult to fully grasp.

288. Original Text:
"မျက်နှာတင်နှောင်"

- *Translation*: "The face rises."

- *Meaning* : Success or recognition brings visibility and pride.

289. Original Text:
"ကျောကြီးမှသင်္ဘော"

- *Translation*: "The boat from the back."

- *Meaning* : Sometimes, it's the unseen or underestimated efforts that lead to success.

290.   Original Text: "မျက်နှာပြင်မှရွှေး"

- *Translation*: "The gold from the surface."

- *Meaning* : The most valuable things are often hidden beneath the surface, requiring effort to uncover.

291.   Original Text: "ဖယ်စင်ခြင်းခံတယ်"

- *Translation*: "Faced with the obstacle."

- *Meaning* : Life presents many obstacles that must be confronted and handled directly.

292.   Original Text: "သုခါတ်သဘော"

- *Translation*: "The boat of wisdom."

- *Meaning* : Wisdom guides the journey through life, just like a boat navigating the waters.

293. Original Text: "အမင်းတော်တစ်ခု"

- *Translation*: "One great achievement."

- *Meaning* : Accomplishing a significant goal or task gives one great pride and satisfaction.

294. Original Text: "ပုံကိုလိုက်အောင်"

- *Translation*: "Follow the pattern."

- *Meaning* : Success often comes from sticking to the right path and following established methods.

295. Original Text: "လေ့လာခြင်းမှလွတ်"

- *Translation*: "Free from learning."
- *Meaning* : Knowledge and growth often require hard work and effort, freeing one from ignorance.

296. Original Text:
"တကယ်တွင်သောသူ"

- *Translation*: "The one who is truly here."
- *Meaning* : Being genuine and present in every moment leads to authenticity and true success.

297. Original Text:
"ကျိုကွဲလေးအမြင်"

- *Translation*: "The shattered view."
- *Meaning* : Life may break into fragments, but it's how we piece things together that counts.

298. Original Text:
"လှုပ်ရှားသောခြေသွား"

- *Translation*: "Moving feet."

- *Meaning* : Constant motion or progress, regardless of speed, will eventually lead to the desired destination.

299. **Original Text:** "အခက်အခဲတွင်အောင်မြင်"

- *Translation*: "Success in difficulty."

- *Meaning* : True success comes when one is able to overcome hardships.

300. **Original Text:** "အကျိုးရှိသောလုပ်ငန်း"

- *Translation*: "A profitable venture."

- *Meaning* : Every effort or task that is approached with care and attention can lead to rewarding outcomes.

THANK YOU

PLEASE DON'T FORGET TO LEAVE A REVIEW

DISCOVER OUR BOOKS COLLECTION:

EDITOR :

LIMITLESS EDITION

https://shorturl.at/1w6Q9

AFRICAN PROVERBS AND SAYINGS

ARABIC PROVERBS AND SAYINGS

CHINESE PROVERBS AND SAYINGS

INDIAN PROVERBS AND SAYINGS

PERSIAN PROVERBS AND SAYINGS

RUSSIAN PROVERBS AND SAYINGS

and more...

DISCOVER

ON AMAZON

KEYSTAR MOON NOTEBOOK COLLECTIONS :

https://shorturl.at/M6juR

ARTWORKS ON SAATCHIART :

https://www.saatchiart.com/en-gb/ye

Happy family
happy kid
Love is gone
Dreamer

Made in United States
Orlando, FL
13 June 2025